End

MW00328264

"A must read for anyone who has experienced the longing for or loss of a child. With candor, humor, and passion, Sandra poignantly shares her tragic journey and the profound healing that can only come from God's amazing grace."

—Kim G., Laguna Niguel, CA

"It is my hope that other women who have faced similar heartache will be encouraged when they read Sandra's story. I am reminded of a verse from the 30th Psalm: 'His favor is for life; weeping may endure for a night, but joy comes in the morning.' God's timing is perfect!"

—Carol C., Jonesboro, GA

"I count it a privilege to endorse Sandra's book and appreciate her courage in writing this. This book is a divine appointment for those who read it."

—Mark Batterson, New York Times bestselling author
of *The Circle Maker*

"From deep places of unimaginable grief, Sandra has written a treasure of hope for anyone crying out to God with an anguished why? I was mesmerized by her story and so thankful for the secrets of grace she offered me."

—Lysa TerKeurst, New York Times bestselling author of *Unglued*
and president of Proverbs 31 Ministries.

Grace Greater Than Our Grief

God's Provision in the
Worst of Times

Sandra DeVane

Hold to His hand
He's holding on to
you —
Sandra DeVane
Isaiah 41:10-13

innovo
PUBLISHING

Published by
Innovo Publishing, LLC
www.innovopublishing.com
1-888-546-2111

Providing Full-Service Publishing Services for
Christian Authors, Artists & Organizations: Hardbacks, Paperbacks,
eBooks, Audiobooks, Music & Film

GRACE GREATER THAN OUR GRIEF
God's Provision in the Worst of Times
Copyright © 2013 Sandra DeVane
All rights reserved.

Scripture marked NASB taken from the New American Standard Bible
Copyright © 1960, 1962, 1963, 1968, 1971, 1972, 1973, 1975, 1977 by The
Lockman Foundation. Used by permission.   Scripture marked NIV taken from
BibleStudyTools.com, New International Version.   Scripture marked RSV taken
from BibleStudyTools.com, Revised Standard Version.   Scripture marked NAS
taken from BibleStudyTools.com, New American Standard.

Library of Congress Control Number: 2013946865
ISBN 13: 978-1-61314-168-7

Cover Design & Interior Layout: Innovo Publishing, LLC

Printed in the United States of America
U.S. Printing History

First Edition: August 2013

Dedicated to Steve DeVane,

the one who walked this road with me

My grace is sufficient for you.

—God

Acknowledgments

This is a simple pencil sketch of events in my life that occurred over a ten-year period; therefore, there's not a lot of detail about other people who played a role in extending God's grace to Steve and me. First of all, there's my mom, Joann Price. Apart from her prayers for me, I know I might still be gasping for air in that miry pit, still searching for that rock to put my feet upon. Along with my dad, Hoke Price, their love, faithfulness, and prayers have carried me through when I knew I could not survive. Even in their own pain—losing grandsons and watching their daughter grieve—they have been a strong tower in my life that I always knew I could run to. Thank you, Mama and Daddy.

There are so many others who have prayed, served, and come alongside us that I know I could never name them all. If your name is missing here, know that God knows who you are and I am grateful.

> Steve's uncle and aunt, Noel and Verie Foster—what a blessing you have been to me. I have counted on your prayers.

> My sisters, Susan and Sherry, and their families

> My brother, Ken, and his wife, Dee

My in-laws, Mike and Dianne

Danny and Merry McMillan

Steve and Renee Clark

The entire BASIC Sunday school class

Parks Davis, my pastor who helped me walk through the valley just by listening and being there

The wonderful people of Jonesboro United Methodist Church

Carol Cook, who diligently read each word and corrected a lot of grammatical errors

All of you who listened to our songs and let us share our words with you

Thank you.

Table of Contents

Introduction

For years, I told this story because I needed to. Today, I tell it once again because so many are in desperate need to hear of God's faithfulness and grace. To hear, as a song once said, "Life is hard, but God is good." To be reminded, this "momentary, light affliction is producing for us an eternal weight of glory far beyond all comparison" (2 Corinthians 4:17, NASB). To be encouraged not to give up but "to keep your eyes fixed on Jesus, the author and perfecter of our faith" (Hebrews 12:2, paraphrased). To be assured that some have gone before you and found "His grace to be sufficient and His power to be made perfect in their weakness" (2 Corinthians 12:9, paraphrased).

I know my story is not the worst thing that could ever happen, but that doesn't matter when it's happening to you. What matters is the answer to the questions: Is there a God? Does He care? Can He get me through this? I want to assure you the answer is yes! I want to do as 2 Corinthians 1:4 says and "comfort you who are in any affliction with the comfort that I received in my affliction" (paraphrased). Most of all, I want those of you who feel like you can't make it one more step to know that, if you believe in Jesus, if you truly trust in Him, when you fall, you will find underneath you His everlasting arms.

No matter what you are facing today, cling to Jesus. Run to the name of the Lord, for that is where you will find your strength. Don't look to other people. Cherish their prayers and receive their love and care, but let your hope and trust be only in God. When Steve and I were first married, I prayed and prayed for a best friend, someone I could share my deepest thoughts with. I couldn't figure out why God wouldn't answer that prayer. It is because He wanted to be that friend, and He has been. He has given me good friends whom I cherish, but He has always been the One I run to first, the One I pour my heart out to without reservation, the One I expect to come through for me. He has never failed me. He cannot.

My prayer for you, my friend, is that you will find Jesus to be your dearest friend, the One who loved you so much that He was willing to lay down His life for you. God is for you. If He gave you His Son, He will give you everything else you may need to face whatever lies ahead in this life. Trust Him. He is worthy of your trust. In the pages that follow, may your hope and faith be renewed in a God who is there, in a God who cares, and in a God whose grace is sufficient for your every need.

1

Roller Coaster

WHAT NO ONE KNEW ABOUT ME, probably not even Steve, was that I wanted a baby. I wanted one badly. I had graduated from college, taught high school for a couple of years, and gotten married—so the next obvious thing was to have a baby. I had recently quit my teaching job, so that was an even better reason to have a baby, right? Steve was working and I was doing whatever came up. I volunteered a lot. I was busy in my church, and I even occasionally substituted for teachers at the local schools when they needed me. That's what I was doing on this particular day. It seemed like any other day, but late in the afternoon I started having pains that began in my lower abdomen that eventually moved to my chest and shot down my left arm. Even though I was only twenty-four, I thought I was having a heart attack. Steve and I were living with his brother, Mike, at the time. I'm not sure Mike knew what to think, but because of my hysteria he decided quickly that he needed to take me to the hospital.

We all got in his car and he sped to the hospital with me screaming in the back seat that I was dying. The surest way to get seen immediately in the emergency room is to walk in bent over holding your chest, shouting, "I'm having a heart attack!" They took me straight back. Turns out I wasn't having a heart attack; I was having a baby, thirty-three weeks too early.

That was the beginning of what would turn out to be a very long and winding road with many potholes, bumps, boring straight-a-ways, and tragic downhills. It was May of 1985. Had I known what the next eight or nine years held, I would have told you I would not be able to endure it. But God's grace carries us through the unimaginable and sets us down gently on the other side.

Not long after the miscarriage I started having this strange pain in my lower abdomen, so I went to the doctor about it. They wound up doing exploratory surgery, thinking they would find nothing, but what they found was a mess. I had an old ectopic pregnancy, an inflamed appendix, and my intestines were tangled up with scar tissue. The doctor cleaned me out and put me back together. The following months and years led to three more miscarriages; numerous doctors, including a top fertility specialist; and several surgeries, with no success at all. It was one disappointment after another.

If having babies is easy for you, what you may not know is that dealing with infertility is one of the most humiliating experiences a woman can have. I won't attempt to speak for all women because I'm aware that people are different. There may be some women who take it in stride but there are others, like me, who say with Jacob's wife, Rachel, "Give me children, or else I die" (Genesis 30:1, NASB). And you die a thousand deaths. Not only the deaths of babies through miscarriage that you will never see until heaven, but the deaths of your dreams, your plans, your ego, your pride, and your relationships. If you know of someone going through this experience, you may think they are breezing through, but that may be a lie.

No one knew the torture I was experiencing. For me, letting someone see how much I wanted something that I couldn't have was more than my pride would allow, and so I kept it hidden except in my crazy moments when it slipped out. My mind became irrational at times, and I thought things that just weren't true. My worth as a person became diminished in my eyes because I couldn't produce a child. I felt like I should park in the handicapped zone; I felt like my parents would love me less because I couldn't give them grandchildren like my siblings; I felt like I had a big sign on me that screamed DEFECTIVE. I had trouble being around people with children. I hated going to baby showers. I hated all the stupid things people would often say, like the time a lady at a baby shower turned to me and said, "Do you have kids?" I said, "No," hoping she would turn her head and not look at me anymore. But she responded, "Do you want mine?" I'm sure she never thought another thing about it. I'm sure it was supposed to be funny.

That's the thing: when you're walking through the valley of infertility, there are no jokes because the joke's on you. You are the joke, and you're tired of being laughed at. Even though no one's laughing, you can feel like the whole world is pointing at you. I suspect many people wonder why married couples in their late twenties, and especially their thirties, don't have kids. Perhaps they wonder, "Is there something wrong with them?"

I vividly remember the day I allowed myself to stay home from a baby shower. It may sound like weakness to those who think you should always think of others and do the right thing, but for me it was a victory. For me, it was finding the voice to say, "This hurts too bad, and I'm not going to pretend anymore that it doesn't." I only remember staying home from one because I rarely cut myself slack, but right or wrong, I really believe God was saying, "It's okay."

2

Samuel

WHEN I WAS JUST ABOUT READY to give up and be content with only being an aunt, I tried one more doctor. He suggested putting me through menopause and then bringing my ovaries back to life. I looked at him and told him politely that if he did anything to me that would make me any more hormonally challenged than I already was, there would be no hope of having a baby because I wouldn't have a husband. He then suggested that he just run some tests. He took some blood and said he'd call with the results. You would think that one of the doctors somewhere along the line would have tested my blood. But they didn't. They should have. It may have saved me months, even years, of heartache. But then again, maybe not. My tests came back showing that my prolactin level was at the level of a breastfeeding mother, so I was probably only rarely ovulating, and my progesterone was so low that if I did happen to get pregnant there was no way my body would maintain it. That's exactly what had been happening. He gave me a pill to adjust my levels, and the next month I got pregnant.

When I was nine weeks pregnant I had an ultrasound. They called and told me there was no baby, that the fetus sac was empty. I didn't even know there was such a thing. They told me I would probably miscarry when my body realized I wasn't pregnant. A couple of weeks later, I still had not miscarried and I went for another ultrasound. Lo and behold, the baby was back! I don't know whether they just missed him the first time or if it was a miracle (I had prayed for one). I was happy either way.

At twelve weeks pregnant, my doctor decided I had an incompetent cervix. To keep me from miscarrying, he put stitches in my cervix to sew it shut and told me I had to be on bed rest for the next twenty-four weeks. What "bed rest"

Life Lesson

If you know people who are shut-in, go visit them, even if it's been too long and you're embarrassed. They will just be glad for the company. It's a lonely world.

turned out to be was not getting out of the bed for more than ten minutes a day. I was not even allowed to sit in a recliner. I had to be flat on my back. Steve and I moved in with my parents because my dad had just retired, and he could wait on me hand and foot during the day while Steve worked. It may sound like "the life" and it might have been if it were only for a couple of weeks, but it was truly awful. I watched TV, cross stitched, made a rug with a hook, did crossword puzzles, read my Bible, read books, cried, prayed, stared, counted time in various ways, and cried some more.

C. S. Lewis said, "Experience: that most brutal of teachers. But you learn, my God do you learn."[1] Some of the things I learned:

- People remember you when your situation is new; after a couple of weeks, they'll go on with their lives.
- The world will go on without you, even if you think you are indispensable.
- TV gets really boring after a couple of weeks.
- Going to the doctor can be exciting, especially if it's the only time you can get out of bed all month.
- My dad thinks a serving of ice cream is half of a half-gallon carton.
- Sometimes having nothing to do is worse than having too much to do.
- Twenty-four weeks is a long time.

---

[1] Brainy Quote, C. S. Lewis, http://www.brainyquote.com/quotes/quotes/c/cslewis103466.html.

At thirty-six weeks, I went to the doctor to get the stitches cut. He assured me I would probably go into labor and have the baby that day. I had the baby six weeks later—yes, I said SIX WEEKS. I was two weeks overdue. Sometimes doctors are wrong. I do not have an incompetent cervix. But at least I had twenty-four weeks to think about it.

I had an 8-pound, 7-ounce baby boy we named Samuel Keene DeVane—Samuel because he was "asked of the Lord." He was healthy, whole, and he was here; that's all that mattered. I guess God wanted us to never doubt that we had a baby after begging Him for so long for one because we certainly never forgot Samuel was around. I had friends who could forget their babies because they were so quiet. Samuel was never quiet. He cried a lot. He screamed a lot. He hated his car seat; he hated the car. He had colic. The baby books we read on how to deal with these issues were not helpful. Samuel did not respond to any of the suggestions in the way the authors said he would. No advice seemed to help. The only thing that calmed him down was the noise from the hair dryer, the tub water being turned on full blast, or the vacuum cleaner. One night, Steve and I turned the hair dryer on, laid it on the dresser, and slept for about four hours. We were desperate.

Samuel was demanding, but he was a delight. He was mischievous and precious and fun. He was my life. All I did was take care of Sam. When Sam was about sixteen months old, Steve and I left him with my mom and dad and went on a weekend retreat on evangelism. When we went to pick up Sam on Sunday afternoon, his cheeks were all red. The next day, I took him to the doctor because he had a rash and was running a fever. They didn't know what was wrong with him. He didn't seem to feel too bad. One doctor said he had the measles but wasn't sure.

On Wednesday evening, he started to get worse; we couldn't get him to go to sleep. He kept hitting the back of his head and had a purple rash on his neck. The doctor gave us a prescription to make him sleep. It didn't work. I had a gut feeling something was wrong and I wanted to demand that someone listen to me, but I was fearful of looking like a paranoid first-time mom. So I suppressed it. After being up all night, I gave him some Tylenol for the fever, and I spilled a little on his leg. Steve was holding him, and I got a rag to wipe it. As soon as I did, he had a seizure. I totally freaked out and started casting out demons. I mean I lost it! Thankfully, Steve had more sense than I did and called 9-1-1. The ambulance came and took Samuel to the hospital. They told us they thought the seizure was from the fever and he would be okay, but they were going to keep him through the night. Steve left to go home, and I stayed with Samuel.

I told the nurses he looked like he was still having seizures. They assured me he wasn't but said they would put him on a monitor just to make me feel comfortable so I could get some sleep. As soon as they hooked up the monitor, it started going off. Pretty soon he was having constant seizures

19

and the nurse called the doctor. He told her to put Dilantin in his IV. As soon as the medicine entered his body, he quit breathing, right there in front of me. The nurse freaked, left the room, and left me standing there watching my son turn blue. I didn't know what to do so I grabbed the hand oxygen pump (called an Ambu bag), put the mask over his mouth and nose, and squeezed the bag. The emergency team came in and demanded to know who I was. When I said, "I'm his mom," they told me to get out. I stood in the hall looking at the ceiling, and screamed to God that if He were real, I was going to find out now!

I didn't know it, but while I was in the hall screaming, Steve was at home praying and God told him to memorize Isaiah 41:13, which says, "For I am the LORD, your God, who takes hold of your right hand and says to you, Do not fear, I will help you" (NIV). We were definitely going to need that promise in the days to come. Someone was going to have to hold our hands and help us or we would not make it.

The lady in the next room let me in, and I called my mom and dad. Daddy answered the phone and I just started crying and said, "Daddy, Sam's dying." It's been over twenty-two years ago, and I still cry thinking about the horror of that night. The hospital sent a chaplain and put me in the room with him. We just sat there with no one talking. When my mom walked in the door, I burst into tears and said, "Mama, God says He works all things together for good for those who love Him. And Mama, I love Him."

The emergency room doctor came and told me they had resuscitated Samuel but that it looked like he had meningitis, and they were going to have to life-flight him to Egleston Children's Hospital. We were at Georgia Baptist Hospital, several miles away. We went over to Egleston and waited. Lots of friends and family came to the hospital and just sat with us. I remember walking down the hall with my sister that day and saying to her, "If this life is all there is, this is a cold, cruel joke."

At about three o'clock Friday afternoon, the doctor came and told us he had pronounced Sam brain dead and with our permission, he would take him off life-support. First, they needed to ask us if they could have Sam's eyes. Samuel had the most beautiful blue eyes. They didn't want any of his other body parts because they didn't know what had killed him. It's a horrible decision to have to make, but you just do the best you can, trusting in God's grace. Perhaps another child has vision today because of Sam, and another set of parents has hope for their child. Although it's

> ## Life Lesson
>
> If you ever wonder if you should go be with someone in a bad situation, even if you have nothing to say, even if you feel awkward, even if they're not your best friend—yes, you should go. They will remember. They will not wonder why you're there. They will be thankful you care.

not something I have taken great comfort in, as some may, at least I can accept it and acknowledge that it is good.

They let us go in the room with him and said once they unplugged the machines I could hold him. No one told me that when people are dead sometimes their muscles still contract and they move. So when Sam's leg pulled up like he was bending it as I started to hold him, I lost it. I thought he was alive. They told me that just happens sometimes. I held him, but I was in shock. It was awful, just awful.

Looking back on that week, I realized I was just going through the motions, letting life hit me in the face without trying to change it. I don't remember praying and asking God to heal Sam. I may have. I'm sure friends and family did. It just happened so fast I didn't really know what was going on. I struggled for months, maybe years, after Samuel died with people who say it was lack of faith. When your child gets a virus, do you usually go into super faith mode and fast and pray? That's all it was, a simple virus. They told us after the autopsy that his immune system had overreacted and blew a fuse, which caused his brain to hemorrhage. One day he had a rash and a fever; two days later he was dead.

MY ANSWER TO PRAYER WAS DEAD.

3

The Funeral

WE LEFT THE HOSPITAL AND WENT to my mom's house. By this time, Steve and I had been up for seventy-two hours, and there was no way we could sleep. The doctor gave us a prescription for Xanax and that helped. My first waking thought the next day, and for weeks after, was, "Sam is dead." Almost every thought and action was preceded by, "Sam is dead."

The next few days were exhausting, but again, the shock carries you through. We stood for hours at the funeral home greeting people—some I remember, and some I don't. I remember the first time I saw Samuel in the casket. I screamed because they had not done his hair right. They had combed his bangs straight down, and he didn't look right. As we stood by the casket, I remember asking my pastor, "How am I ever going to close it?" I really had no clue, but like most things, God's grace carries you along—it's never there before you need it, but it's there when you do.

I was so hurt, and it felt like people's words were cutting me. One day, I threw sympathy card after sympathy card across the room in a fit of anger. I was furious that anyone thought my memories could sustain me. I decided that people who wrote those cards had never lost anything of value. I didn't want memories; I wanted my son. The sentiment, "It's the thought that counts," is difficult for those who are grieving. But at some point, I needed to believe it to stay sane. There is so much room for misunderstanding and taking offense. The hard truth is that the one grieving has to eventually be able to extend the same amount of mercy he or she received to those who seek to help. One of my favorite cards was one I received from my sister's next-door neighbor. It had a check for $50 in it and just said, "I am so sorry. I cannot imagine what you're going through, but sometimes I just need to go shopping." I don't know why it blessed me so much; it wasn't the money. Maybe it was just someone reaching out and trying to feel my pain and heal it in a concrete way. Now when I send sympathy cards, I never get one that says anything about memories sustaining the person even though that might be of comfort to them. It didn't comfort me. My favorite cards are ones that say something like, "Hearts speak when words cannot—just want you to know I care."

> *Life Lesson*
>
> When someone loses a loved one, most of the time, the best thing to say is just, "I'm sorry."

24

Steve looked at me at some point in all of this and said, "I thought I'd had my one tragedy for life but I guess I was wrong." When Steve was eighteen, two years before we married, he was in a car wreck that killed his mom, dad, and grandmother. He was the only survivor. Now he had survived his only son. Some things just ought not be.

> *Life Lesson*
>
> Should you go to the funeral or visitation even if you don't know the person well? Absolutely. It matters that you care. It matters that you're there.

I don't remember a lot about the funeral. I remember we sang a couple of my favorite hymns: "How Firm a Foundation" and "It Is Well with My Soul." I remember my pastor, Parks Davis, talked about Sam and how much he liked balls. We buried him with several of his favorite balls. He loved balls. I remember feeling such a presence of the love of God, especially when the funeral director helped me in the car to go to the burial site. When I looked at him, I just felt God's love for him flowing through me. I didn't say anything but later I wished I had told him how much God loved him.

About three weeks after the funeral, Steve and I went on a weekend trip to Callaway Gardens with some dear friends, Kim and Kurt. They were easy to be around, probably partly because they were struggling with their own grief. It had been a wonderful day, full of enjoying God's creation and the presence and comfort of friends. But that evening, the grief began to close in, and I just had to get away. I went to my room early, got my Bible, and just starting searching through the "Balm of Gilead," looking for something to soothe my soul. I came to Isaiah 61:1, 3:

> The Spirit of the Lord GOD is upon me, because the LORD has anointed me to bring good news to the afflicted;

> He has sent me to bind up the brokenhearted . . . to grant those who mourn in Zion, giving them a garland instead of ashes, the oil of gladness instead of mourning, the mantle of praise instead of a spirit of fainting. So they will be called oaks of righteousness, the planting of the LORD, that He may be glorified.

God spoke so clearly to me—I was His planting for the display of His glory. This is good news: to know that you have not been forgotten; that your life has a purpose; that Jesus came to heal your broken heart and to clothe you with praise in exchange for your spirit of heaviness; to turn what looks like a pile of ashes into something beautiful; and to know that one day you will dance again with joy.

A couple of months before Sam died, I had been reading A. W. Tozer's book, *Pursuit of God*.[2] There is a prayer you can pray at the end of one of the chapters that says something like, "God, make heaven more real to me than any earthly thing has ever been." I prayed that prayer. God answered it. There had to be a heaven, Samuel had to be there, and I had to believe I would see him again someday. That was the only way I would survive. The Apostles' Creed also took on new life for me, especially where it says, "I believe in the RESURRECTION OF THE BODY" (emphasis added). On Sunday mornings, I wanted to recite that bit just a little louder.

---

[2] A. W. Tozer, *The Pursuit of God*, http://www.gutenberg.org/catalog/world/readfile?fk_files=3277609&pageno=25

4

Everything Changes

IT TOOK ABOUT THREE WEEKS FOR the shock to wear off. It was long enough for most everyone else's life to go back to normal and for me to realize that mine never would. Everywhere I went the thing that struck me was how normal and unaffected everyone else seemed. At the grocery store one day, I looked around and wanted to scream, "PLEASE STOP! Do you realize that my son just died?" It was so hard to process the fact that my world had been devastated, and for everyone else it was business as usual. I had a deep need for everyone to know what I was going through. I wanted to show strangers pictures of Samuel and tell them he died—not to shock them but just so they could acknowledge him. It made things awkward because others felt like they had to say or do something to help when all I really wanted was for Samuel to matter; I couldn't tell the details of what happened enough. I know people got tired of hearing it, and others who might have wanted to hear were afraid to ask, but I needed to tell it.

While there is no "one size fits all" when it comes to grief and loss, sometimes a person is just waiting for someone to ask about his or her situation or loved one. Talking about it sometimes helps because it gives the experience meaning and the person value. It can also relieve the tension and awkwardness of the moment. Be led by the Spirit, of course, but sometimes asking about it and offering your sympathy is better than staring at the elephant in the room.

> ### *Life Lesson*
> Don't ever be afraid to ask someone about a loved one who has died, especially if they make mention of them first. Most likely, they would love an opportunity to tell you.

Sam died on November 16, so Christmas was just around the corner. In fact, my dad had already bought him a little red wagon that he had to return. In many ways, it was the most difficult Christmas of my life. I did my best to hold it together and enjoy family and friends with a gaping hole in my life and heart. On the other hand, it was the most meaningful Christmas I had ever celebrated because I was so thankful that Jesus had been born. Jesus, our hope of eternal life—the One who takes away the sting of death.

All my relationships changed because who I was had changed. I could no longer share a bond with my friends who had small children. I remember one friend getting angry with me that Sam had died because, as she said, "You ruined everything." People say strange things. But what I've had to learn over the years is that when something like this happens, it affects everyone in your life, not just you. People may become angry with you because you don't act the way they think you should. One friend came to me years later to ask my forgiveness for being angry with me for so long because when Sam died, I shut her out. I was shocked to hear that from her because I didn't realize that's what I did, but she's right. I probably did. At the time, I was just trying to survive, and it was the only way I knew how.

C. S. Lewis said, "I never knew grief felt so much like fear."[3] That's the best description I've ever read of what I felt for weeks and months after Sam died. It was an almost suffocating fear. Some days I was scared to death I would not survive, and others I was scared to death I would have to go on living without him. I read book after book written by people who had experienced grief. I clung to God like my life depended on it and believe me, it did. I think I can honestly say that some of those days were the closest I have ever felt to God, and in many ways, the freest I have ever been—I had nothing to prove to Him. I had spent so many years trying to show Him how much I loved Him, and I felt like He said to me, "Stop trying so hard to prove you love Me and let Me love you for a while." I knew that if God was not real and He did not carry me through, I would not make it. There was

---

[3] C. S. Lewis, *A Grief Observed* (New York: Seabury, 1961).

no pretending. I remember telling a friend at one point that if God told me He would give me Sam back but He would have to take back all He had shown me of Himself, I would have to say no.

Not everything God said to me at that time in my life was pleasant. One day as I was reveling in self-pity, I picked up my Bible and read in 1 Corinthians 7:30 where it says "Let those who mourn live as though they don't mourn" (paraphrased). I immediately said, "Lord, not fair." Then I flipped over a few pages and read, "And he died for all, that those who live might live no longer for themselves but for him who for their sake died and was raised" (2 Corinthians 5:15, RSV). It was a very difficult Word, but it turned out to be my salvation. If God had not insisted through His Word that I deny myself and live for Him, I would have died or at least been a cripple for the rest of my life.

Some days, I wanted to die. Many days, I drove down the road contemplating the next tree and just running into it. That's one of the things about grief: nothing is constant. One day you feel like you're doing well and actually making progress, and the next you may feel like you're back at the beginning. Grief is not a straight line but more of a circle. You keep going around and around, always coming back to the thoughts and emotions that you thought you'd already defeated. Fortunately, the circles get smaller and the time you spend in each phase gets shorter each time around. I don't know what the experts say, but I wouldn't expect anyone who's had a major loss in his or her life to be "back to normal" before at least two years. That doesn't mean you can't function, and it doesn't mean you will eventually be over it. It just means the grieving process, especially the part where you have to make a conscious choice to go on without the loved one, takes a long time, a lot longer than most people want to allow for.

I remember well the day I had to make the decision to go on living without Sam. It felt like betrayal. It was one of the hardest things I ever had to do, but it was essential. My journal entry from March 4, 1991 tells it all:

> I am at a very hard place in this grieving process. I am angry and rebellious. I am, in a sense, full of rage. I have this incredible urge to throw things, to break something, to hurt and to be hurt. I suddenly realized that I don't really want to choose to be happy anymore because to do that is to accept being without Samuel. That hurts so bad—so bad. I realize I only have two choices: 1) I can live in the past where Samuel is (as far as this life is concerned), or 2) I can leave him and go on in this life without him. Everything in me screams "NO!" I am stuck! I really have no choice at all and that makes me angry! I did not choose to be faced with this choice, if

that makes sense. I don't want to choose, so
I become angry instead. I am acting childish,
but I feel helpless.

I had to decide to leave Samuel with God and go on and live my life. That decision you make to go on with your life is not the end of grief, but it is key to moving forward in the grieving process. I realized later that there are parts of grief that spill into your life for years to come and you only see them when you realize you are healed. Like the day it dawned on me that I no longer had to tell people my story. For years after Sam died, I had to get that part of me in the conversation with someone early on because it was so much a part of who I was. It was an event in my life that marked me forever, but I did not need anyone to know that about me to be whole.

I remember one day going out to Samuel's grave and just sitting there talking to God. At one point, I considered asking God to raise him from the dead. I thought about it for a long time, but didn't do it. I was honestly afraid He might

> ### *Life Lesson*
>
> Don't compare God's ways in your life with anyone else's. Think about when Jesus had just told Peter how he was going to die. Peter looked back at John and asked Jesus, "What about him?" Jesus told Peter, "Don't worry about him, you follow me!" (John 21:18–23, paraphrased).

answer if I did, and then what would I do?

> **Life Lesson**
>
> Some of God's greatest blessings are disguised as disasters.

We had a guy come out to the house so we could order Samuel's headstone. He was a Christian, which I thought was a good thing. By the time he left, I was ready to throw him out of my house. He started telling us about how his little boy had burned his foot. He laid hands on it, prayed, and God healed it. My attitude was an extremely sarcastic: "Yay for him!" It took me a while to let people celebrate their miracles without taking it as a personal attack.

About the same time that Sam died, Steve was in the process of losing his job. He had been working for a savings and loan back during the country's financial crisis. Thankfully, it led to Steve getting a job with Chick-fil-A. He has been there for over twenty years.

5

Us

I READ ONCE THAT 85 PERCENT OF MARRIAGES end in divorce when there is the death of a child. I imagine it might be even higher if that was the couple's only child. The grace of God was the glue that held us; nothing else would have been strong enough. We were both grieving, but we did it differently. Grief didn't draw us together; we went our separate ways, both doing whatever to survive. I don't remember many details, but I do remember just wanting to be happy and to be with someone who made me feel good. There was a season where I felt justified in that feeling, until one night when I had told Steve that I didn't love him anymore, and then I went to church. The pastor taught on 1 Corinthians 13. I don't know what he said, but I know what God said to me. "If you think the love in your marriage has failed, then what you think is love is not love because love never fails." That was it. I went home, fell on my face, and asked God to forgive me and show me how to love. I'm not sure I've learned, but I'm still here and so is Steve. I wrote him a song one day to show him that I was staying—he could count on it.

COUNT ON ME

I have so often taken you for granted
An orphan at 18, a husband at 20
I am the one who receives the most attention
But you are the one who's attended to me

You've held me in your arms like a child
You've cherished every tear that I've cried
You've waited and you've loved me
As I've had to learn the hard way
But after all these years
You're still here
And you'll stay and I'll stay
Work it out
Work it through,
Oh you'll stay and I'll stay
Count on me, baby
'Cause I sure count on you

I have so often expected perfection
As if I myself had reached it somehow
You tiptoed lightly to prevent an insurrection
Hopefully honey, I'm more humble now

You've held me in your arms like a child
You've cherished every tear that I've cried
You've waited and you've loved me
As I've had to learn the hard way
But after all these years
You're still here
And you'll stay and I'll stay
Work it out
Work it through
Oh you'll stay and I'll stay
Count on me, baby
'Cause I sure count on you

A sure case for grace this marriage will be
A case for grace this woman too
It's a good thing I didn't marry me
It's a good thing I married you
'Cause you'll stay . . .

Steve and I have been married for twenty-nine years. When we said, "I do" so many years ago, we both believed what our church taught, that marriage is a sacred covenant and should not be entered into lightly. The fact that we chose to enter into a covenant with each other, before God, has kept us together at times when nothing else would have. Today, I thank God for the power of His grace to fulfill a promise. I know if either of us had gone off to find happiness in someone else, we might have found a season of pleasure and relief, but we would have left a trail of brokenness behind and inside both of us.

6

Caleb

WE WERE MAKING PROGRESS IN OUR grief. I had started working at our church as the youth minister. Teenagers surrounded us, and most days were okay. There were still those days when the tears would come out of nowhere and I would think, *Wow! Will I ever be normal?* By this time, I had decided I could be content without a child. However, in April of 1992, almost a year and a half after Sam died, I found out I was pregnant again. On Sam's birthday, July 23, we went to have an ultrasound. The doctor held up an ultrasound picture. He said, "This is a normal baby. I know because it's my son." He then picked up another one and said, "This is your baby, and it is not normal. There is not enough amniotic fluid. This baby's kidneys have not formed properly, and he will not live."

I don't remember my exact reaction, but I did think it was a very poor way to inform someone their baby was not going to live. I was in shock again. I had just started to get my theological house of cards rebuilt, and this just blew them all down again. I don't think I cried until I got home and called my mom. As soon as I started to tell her, I burst into tears. Looking back, I wonder if I should have gone into desperate prayer mode, seeking out people with the gift of healing. I didn't. Again, I'm sure my family and friends were praying, but I think by this point I felt so beat up that most of my energy was spent surviving and trying to hold my faith together. I had this weird thought that I needed to protect God's reputation and that if I didn't hold it together, people might think less of God. You know the old, "you are the only Bible that some people will ever read" theology. That is true on some levels, but I've learned that it does not mean you should fake it. God is real and we should be too. Sometimes real isn't pretty. I'm not saying lose all self-control and sin, but let God be God, and for you, be scared out of your mind if that's what you feel. I do remember the basic Gospel being extremely clear to me at this point. I told my sister one day that the only thing I knew right then was that the Gospel was true—Jesus Christ died for my sins, rose again, and I would live forever. Sometimes when life is too complicated to figure out all of the whys, just simply believing the Gospel is good.

There were other days when I didn't know what I believed. It had been two weeks since we found out. I don't remember what started it but the phrase from the Old Testament "rent their clothes," as in "tearing them in grief," came to life for me. Steve and I were sitting at the kitchen table talking, and I got so angry that I picked up a full glass of iced tea and threw it across the room. It hit the door and shattered into a thousand pieces; sweet tea went everywhere. Then I took the collar of the new maternity shirt I had on and with both hands ripped it in two. Then I stood up and yelled, "What kind of God are You? You want the glory when things go good and the glory when they go bad!"

Another time, I was riding in the car with Steve and in my mind I began to say, "I hate You God!" It really surprised me because I had been the perfectly humble Christian lately, or so I thought. I got home and fell on my face and began reading the last few chapters of Job. It was at that point that I could say with Job, "I had heard of You with the hearing of the ear; But now my eye sees You; Therefore I retract, And I repent in dust and ashes" (Job 42:5–6, NAS). I realized that night that God could do whatever He wanted with me, and my response was to humble myself before Him. We have to choose what we are going to do when God doesn't act like we think He should. Like the disciples in John, sometimes we have to look at Jesus and say, "I will follow You because where else can I go? You alone have the words of eternal life, and I have come to believe that You are the Holy One of God" (John 6:68–70, paraphrased).

I WILL FOLLOW YOU

When the road gets hard and it's hard to believe
When my concept of who You are
Has gone crazy on me
When the words You say are so hard to hear
When the things that You allow
Make You seem so severe
I will follow You
I will follow You
I'll follow You.

When the things I ask and the things You do
Seem to fix a gulf between what I want
And what is true
When I am afraid and I feel like You don't care
When all my senses scream at me
That You are just not there
I will follow You
I will follow You
I'll follow You.

'Cause where else can I go?
You're the only One I know
Who else has the words of eternity?
Where else can I run when I have come to believe
And You are life to me?

When my thoughts get confused and my soul is weary
When finally I'm drawn into Your sanctuary
When You take my hand and You make me sure
That though my heart and flesh may fail
Your love for me endures
I will follow You
I will follow You
I'll follow You.

Some people thought I should go ahead and abort the baby since he wasn't going to live anyway, but I couldn't do that. I carried him a little over three months after I found out that, short of a miracle, he would die at birth. I went into labor and called my doctor, who happened to be on vacation. He forgot to tell the doctor on call about me, so when I arrived at the hospital, they didn't think I knew what I was talking about. They put me on a monitor and told me the baby's heart was strong. I tried to tell them it wasn't his heart. The on-call doctor told me about a couple who was told their baby wouldn't live but the doctors were wrong. It was frustrating more than helpful. I had been carrying the baby around with me night and day without amniotic fluid. I could feel all of his body parts because there was no cushioning. I rarely slept for fear that I was hurting him. Now the day had come, and the doctors wanted to tell me maybe they were wrong?

They put me in the delivery room and couldn't get my epidural to work. They gave me tons of narcotics and then finally gave me an epidural on the other side because they couldn't get it to cross over my spine. My doctor came back from his trip in time to deliver the baby. I knew he was alive in me but as soon as I delivered him, I was sure he would die. No, I had no faith that he would live. I had had so many disappointments that hope scared me.

The baby was born and he lived for an hour. We held him and named him Caleb. Our pastor baptized him. One of the worst things about that night was that not long after he was born, they came in the middle of the night, woke me up, and told me they had to move me to a regular room since Caleb had died. Only people with babies could stay in the labor and delivery rooms. Someone without an ounce of compassion made that decision. It was like the straw, and I was the camel.

I wrote a letter to Caleb after he was born. The hospital staff asked me for a copy of it so they could share it with mothers who had lost their babies.

Dear Caleb,

When I first learned of your new life in me, I was surprised, yet very happy. The others had been so long in coming and you just appeared. I no longer needed a child to make me whole, but I wanted one to love very much. I loved you almost immediately.

When I first learned that something had gone wrong and that short of a miracle you had no chance at life apart from me I was sad, but not really surprised. I guess, unfortunately, I've grown accustomed to bad news. But I still continued to love you, and as you grew, my love for you grew.

When you were born, I was afraid. But one look at your face took my fear away. I saw you and called you "Caleb" in my heart. Caleb had a different spirit according to God and you did too. I held you and wished I could hold you forever, but I knew I had to give you back.

Others think your life was a waste and that it didn't matter. Some may think that the ordeal was only suffering, but I know better. Forgive me for the times I complained. I didn't know what I was doing. But now that I've seen your face and held you in my arms I can honestly say, it was worth it and I'd do it again.

Even though you only lived for an hour, you are still my son. I will always remember you. I will call you by your name because you are important. And Caleb, I will love you forever.

Someone once said, "'Tis better to have loved and lost than never to have loved at all." Thank you, God, for giving me the chance to love another son. I don't understand much, but I'm still asking to love and trust You with all my heart. I don't understand why Caleb died, but I pray that his life will somehow bring You glory and that Steve's and my response will do the same.

> *"Our joys will be greater,*
> *Our love will be deeper*
> *Our life will be fuller*
> *Because we shared your moment."*

I came home from the hospital and rested a few days, but because I didn't have a baby, I decided to go back

> ### *Life Lesson*
>
> The Bible teaches us that God's grace is sufficient. It is. But sometimes we must remember that bread and water are sufficient to sustain life. We don't need a steak dinner, though we may want one. God's grace is sufficient but it doesn't necessarily go down like a gourmet meal at a fancy restaurant.

to work. I went to my office but soon told the secretary that I didn't feel well, thought I might have the flu, and went home. That illness lingered; it came and went. I went from doctor to doctor, some telling me I had Lyme disease and others wanting to give me an antidepressant. Finally, a rheumatologist told me I had fibromyalgia. He looked me in the eye and said, "The good news is that it won't kill you. The bad news is that you will have it the rest of your life." The bad news today is that I've never really felt good since, and it's been over twenty years. I've fought it constantly. I've occasionally looked for answers. I've changed my diet a hundred times but without enough success to matter. I make myself exercise. I don't know if the combination of months without sleep, years of stress without relief, and a double epidural and tons of drugs right at birth just did something terrible to me, but I would love to go back and undo whatever it was. Steve is the only one who really knows how difficult it is sometimes. It's not that I can't do what needs to be done and a lot of what I want to do—it's just rare that I really feel like doing it. But God's grace is sufficient, and there's never been a time when I haven't been able to do what He wanted done.

7

Music

STEVE AND I HAD ALWAYS BEEN involved in music. We sang in the choir at church. He played the guitar for me to sing solos on occasion. I had been a voice performance major for one quarter at the University of Georgia and Steve had been a music major for a quarter also. During the years of grief and loss, I had spent hours depressed and writing. I started playing some chords on the piano just so I could write songs. I wrote a lot of songs. They may not have been the best songs, but they were meaningful to me. We started getting together with some friends and eventually began to go around to churches and other venues to share our music and testimony. The first song I ever wrote was a song called, "You'd Follow Me" based on Psalm 139:

YOU'D FOLLOW ME

It's so wonderful how You love me
Even when I don't understand
It's so wonderful how You woo me
Oh, I'm not worthy, I'm not worthy.

How low will You go
To follow Your sheep who's lost her way?
How high will You go to bring her back to reality?
If I take the wings of the morning
To the uttermost parts of the sea
You'd follow me, Oh—I know You
You'd follow me.

How dark can it get
And You still be the light of my way?
How long will You burn
And be with me as bright as the day?
If I say let the darkness cover me
And let the light around me be as night
You'd shine on me like a bright light
You'd follow me, Oh—I know You
You'd follow me.

I wrote my second song about my nephew who had been born with a birth defect. Life was difficult for him, and it broke my heart. One day, I found out that his name meant "Healer," and the thought occurred to me that we could all find some healing in him if we could love.

HEALING CHILD

I remember when you were born
We were all so afraid
How could such a small one survive such pain?
I remember how I cried, almost died, to see your scars
But they were nothing
Compared to what the world would bring.

And today I still cry
Until my eyes are dry
'Cause I know the world is hard, so hard on you.
Oh, what can I do to make you smile?
My healing Child.

Today I look at you and I see scars
Of a different kind
They may not hurt your body
But they've hurt your mind
As far as I can see, this old world lacks a lot of love
And I'm so afraid we don't love enough.

I still pray for your healing and I look for it each day
But now I see through different eyes, a different truth
Maybe we've all found some healing in you.

And today I still cry
Until my eyes are dry
'Cause I know the world is hard, so hard on you.
Oh, what can I do to make you smile?
My healing Child.

For several years, we sang and shared. Many people heard our story and hopefully many were blessed and found some healing themselves. But most of it was probably for us. My mom said once, "Sandra needs to sing." And that was true—God used the music to heal me most of all.

Some of the songs were cathartic like the one called, "I Keep Coming Back to You." One thing I could not bear were people who seemed to have all the answers at a time when my world didn't make a bit of sense. I've since learned that if I humble myself, I can love those people too, but at the time I was just angry. All I knew was that I would keep coming back to the Lord because even though I didn't know much, I knew He was the answer and I would find all I needed in Him. I wrote some words and Steve put them to music.

I KEEP COMING BACK TO YOU

Some people seem to have it all together
And honestly it wearies me to meet up with their kind
'Cause if I ever got it all together
I'd probably pack it up and lose it in my mind.

So I keep coming back to You, Lord
With nothing in my hands and even less in my heart
I keep coming back to You, Lord
Praying for mercy and a brand-new start.

Some people seem to have all the answers
And usually they feel free to tell you every one
But if I know nothing else surely I know this
You give me the answer and You give it in Your Son.

So I keep coming back to You, Lord
With nothing in my hands and even less in my heart
I keep coming back to You, Lord
Praying for mercy and a brand-new start.

I try to walk away when times get tough
When "why's" the only question
And the only answer is to trust.

I have included some of my songs in my book because they help tell the story. I pray God uses the words to bring comfort and encouragement to your soul.

8

Merry

A BOOK ABOUT THIS TIME IN my life would not be complete without telling you about Merry. Three months after Samuel died, my pastor, Parks, called and asked if I would sing at a baby's funeral. After thinking about it for a while, I called him back and said I would. The baby had died at seven months from a heart condition. I didn't know the family, but as I was singing, I noticed the mother on the front row looking so weary. Later that week, I called her and asked if she wanted to get coffee. She did. We became friends and still are. She has been a lifesaver through the years. There are just some things that only people who have had a similar experience can understand, and those things can create life-long bonds.

God knew I needed a friend like Merry. I'm not the easiest person in the world to be friends with; I tend to be a loner. I forget that I need people, but Merry was just always there. I took her friendship for granted, I'm sure, for many years but we have been through some tough things and she's hung in there with me. She helped me with the youth when I was pregnant with Caleb, and she was pregnant at the same time. Her son, Nathan, was born the same day we buried Caleb. She left Caleb's burial service and went straight to the hospital. To say that things between us were awkward would be an understatement. Looking back on it now, if Merry had not been who she was, we probably would not still be friends. It was hard to be around her with her baby. Her arms were full and mine were excruciatingly empty. It was years before I realized how difficult that experience must have been for her, and how it would have been so much easier for her to walk away and not keep seeking me out. One evening, she brought some kids over to visit me, and I asked them to leave. Yes, it was rude, but at the moment I didn't care. I later apologized and sent everyone a card but a weaker person than Merry would have written me off. I've probably written people off for lesser things.

Merry's husband, Danny, played in our band so we were together almost constantly for years. We don't live near one another anymore, but I believe our friendship is such that it doesn't matter. She loves me, I love her, and as trite as that may sound, it's really all that matters.

I remember the day she called and told me that Nathan had been hit by a car and taken by helicopter to Egleston Children's Hospital. He was thirteen years old, and they didn't expect him to live. When I got off the phone,

I let out a gut-wrenching scream. It felt like a part of me was dying. She was like my sister and her children belonged to me in that way. I immediately went to the hospital and stayed with her off and on for many days and weeks while we watched God do a miracle. The boy the doctors initially said would most likely be in a vegetative state if he lived is now in college. Yay God!

9

Again

ALMOST A YEAR AFTER CALEB WAS born, I found myself pregnant again. I can't remember much about that time. I was still working full time as the youth minister. It wasn't until I was about seven months pregnant that I began to freak out. By this point, it was obvious I was going to have a baby and there was no turning back. I became depressed and almost paralyzed with fear until I could hardly get out of bed some days.

One morning as I lay in bed wrestling with my fear and depression, I began to think about when the disciples were in the boat and Jesus told Peter to walk to Him on the water. I thought how Peter was doing great but began to sink when he looked around at his situation. That was me. I was sinking. Then I realized that Peter cried out, "Save me, Lord!" and Jesus did just that! He didn't get mad and say, "Swim back, you worthless piece of trash." Jesus took his hand and helped him. That revelation got me out of bed that day and led to a song because I realized God wasn't mad at me for struggling with my faith—His understanding is infinite. If we just cry out, He will save us. He may rebuke us for our little faith, but He will save us, still.

SAVE ME, STILL

Didn't want to get out of bed this morning
Feeling like I'd let You down
Along with everybody else
Seems like I should know by now how to fight this feeling
Seems like if I could lead the blind,
I could help myself.

Oh—Save me, Jesus
Help me before I drown
My eyes can't seem to focus anywhere but down
Oh me of little faith, rebuke me if You will
But save me, Jesus
Save me, Still.

Finally fought my way into the shower
Satan's whispers flood my soul
Like this water flowing over me
Seems like I should know by now that You love me so

Seems like if I could understand
I could just let go.

I just want to follow You
No matter what the cost
I just want to do Your will
But sometimes I feel lost.

Oh—Save me, Jesus
Help me before I drown
My eyes can't seem to focus anywhere but down
Oh me of little faith, rebuke me if You will
But save me, Jesus
Save me, Still.

Steve and I went to a worship service one Sunday morning while I was still wrestling with the fear of having a baby. I believe God illuminated this Scripture for me: "Forget the former things; do not dwell on the past. See, I am doing a new thing!" (Isaiah 43:18–19, NIV). This rarely happens to me, but it was one of those times when you know God is speaking to you personally.

Around the same time, we had gone to dinner with a pastor friend, Randy, and his wife, Chris. As we drove down the road, some friends of theirs pulled up beside our car and told them they had a "Word from the Lord" for the lady in the back seat. Our friend pulled into a bank parking lot and we all got out. The lady looked at me and said, "The Lord wants me to tell you that you are walking around with your head down in unbelief, and He wants you to believe what He has said to you." She went on to say that she believed Satan had stolen our children in an effort to destroy the ministry that God had for us and that she wasn't sure but thought God was saying there would be another child after this one. At that point, I laughed out loud. I know this woman didn't know me, but if I lived through this birth there would definitely not be another. I was finished as far as I was concerned.

We got back in the car and Randy asked what we thought. His advice for when someone said they had a Word from the Lord was to receive what matched with your spirit and discard the rest. She was right about the unbelief; I didn't know about the other. I was pretty sure she just made up the part about another baby.

10

Sally

ON JUNE 7, 1994, SALLY JOANN was born. She was healthy and beautiful. But as soon as I looked into her beautiful blue eyes, I knew holding her for an hour, sixteen months, or a lifetime would never be enough for me. I wanted forever.

I WANT FOREVER

I stare across the sky so blue
Like your eyes melting into view
And my heart heaves with a longing
Oh, to hold you again
But it would never be enough
Once is never enough
I want forever.

I never even got to know you
Your life melted with my view
But even if I could have held you
Oh, for more than just one hour
It would never be enough
Once is never enough
I want forever.

What a cold, cold thought
If this is all there is
What a cruel, cruel world
Unless Jesus really lives.

I look into your eyes so blue
I draw you close for a better view
And my heart leaps with the joy
Your living brings to me
But it could never be enough
Once is never enough
I want forever.

We were made to live forever
But sin took its toll
But love has left this longing in my soul
I want forever, I want forever
Once is not enough for love
Once is not enough for you
I want, I want forever.

When Sally was only two months old, she began to run a fever and vomit. We took her to the hospital and they ran tests and did a spinal tap, just like with Sam. I called my dad and told him it was déjà vu. It turned out to be a kidney infection, and we had to stay at the hospital for seven days with Sally hooked to IVs. During that time, I had a lot of time to sit, think, and read. At some point, I realized that because life had been going smoothly, I had slacked off in my relationship with Jesus. I wrote some words that Steve later put to music that said what I was thinking.

THANK YOU

Some may despise this hour
For all the sadness and pain it brings
Others may be bitter
Wondering why it ever came
But as I sit here in the quiet
With my mind just set on You
I can thank You for the peace
I can thank You for the tears
Just the same.

Thank You
Oh, thank You
For showing me my need
Thank You, Oh, thank You

For being faithful
Faithful to bring me to my knees.

I've seen my dreams die more than one time
And more than twice I've been afraid
Many times You've seemed silent
I've often felt alone when I've prayed
But as I sit here I still know
That fear itself has been my friend
It's drawn me to You
And I've found You faithful to the end.

Thank You
Oh, thank You
For showing me my need
Thank You, Oh, thank You
For being faithful
Faithful to bring me to my knees.

Sally pulled through that experience and has grown up to be a very lovely young lady. She has been such a blessing to us and has taught me so much about the love of God for His children. I was holding her one night—just amazed at how much I could love her—and God spoke to me about His love for me. That's been something that's hard for me to abide in, but God has used my children and my husband to teach me well.

BECAUSE YOU'RE MINE

I hold you while you're sleeping,
Can't believe the love I feel
So tenderly I touch you as my heart begins to kneel
As a sparkling revelation like light upon your brow
Finds a home within my soul as quietly God shouts—

I am Love and you are loved
Just like you love this child
I am Love and you are loved
This revelation could drive the kingdom wild
My nature is to love you, Oh learn of Love divine
I don't love you 'cause you're perfect
I love you 'cause you're Mine.

Souls in desperation, they try so hard to cope
Everywhere are answers but it seems there's little hope
Oh please let me tell you what I have found is true
There's a God who is longing to say these words to you.

I am Love and you are loved
Just like you love this child
I am Love and you are loved
This revelation could drive the kingdom wild
My nature is to love you, Oh learn of Love divine
I don't love you 'cause you're perfect
I love you 'cause you're Mine.

11

Anna

I SUPPOSE THE LADY WHO PROPHESIED to me in the bank parking lot was right—I did have another baby. Her name is Anna Lynne. I named her Anna because the prophetess Anna, who welcomed Jesus in the temple, has always fascinated me. When I was pregnant with her, they ran some tests because I was over thirty-five and considered "high-risk." The doctor called one day and told me that the results of one of the tests showed a high probability that the baby would have Down syndrome. Steve told me to tell them to do the test again, and he began to fast. He told me he was going to fast and pray until the results came back. While he was fasting, one day I met a friend for lunch at Applebee's. While we were there, the lady from the bank parking lot came walking by my table. We didn't know each other, but I recognized her from the last time she prophesied to me. She walked by my table and back to her seat. It was strange to me because our table was up a couple of stairs in an elevated section of the restaurant, and her seat was in a completely different section. I couldn't figure out why she would come up there. I don't know if that had anything to do with it, but four days later the test results came back very different from before; there was absolutely no problem with the baby.

Anna was born healthy with the longest blonde hair you have probably ever seen on a baby. Some of it was already down to her chin. She was beautiful and precious, and I knew God had great things in store for her. I realized one day that Sally and Anna were both born on Tuesday. I remember hearing that Tuesday's children are children of grace. Of course, that led me to write a song about them.

SALLY & ANNA'S SONG

The brightest blue eyes, the blondest long hair
Two girls that brighten our lives 'cause they're there
Both Tuesday's children and filled with His grace
No simple chance brought you two to this place.

Jesus, Jesus
You're the One we must teach them to trust
Jesus, Jesus,
Help us to love them the way
You love us.

A gift from the Lord, our hearts can't express
The joy that He's given inside this address
We dare not possess but cherish we do
And teach them with all of our hearts to love You.

Jesus, Jesus
You're the One we must teach them to trust
Jesus, Jesus,
Help us to love them the way
You love us.

12

No Regrets

WHEN WE ARE GOING THROUGH DIFFICULT circumstances, it's hard to see any value in them because there's so much fear and misery. But what a blessing when we look back and we see God's faithfulness, the sufficiency of His grace, and how He has used each and every thing to make us more like Jesus and to comfort other people. One of my favorite Scriptures is in 2 Corinthians 1 where it talks about how we receive God's comfort in our trials so that we can comfort others in their afflictions. None of us really want to be spoiled Christians who have never had to struggle and have nothing to offer those who do, but neither do any of us really want to suffer. It's a good thing it's not our choice.

I would have never given my son to die, but I know One who did, and He is the One who makes beauty from ashes, who gives a garment of praise for a spirit of heaviness, and dancing for mourning. He's the One of whom Joseph said in Genesis 50 meant all of his suffering for good, even if those who were responsible meant it for evil.

I struggled for a long time trying to answer the question *why?* especially when a lady told me it was a shame my son had to die before I learned that I had authority over Satan. Did Satan steal my children like the bank lady said? I still have unanswered questions, but this I know—God meant it for good, to bring about the salvation of many people, just as Joseph said.

Life is hard; babies die; and disease, sickness, and tragedy surrounds us on every side. We can live our lives in fear of what might happen to us and our loved ones, or we can choose to believe God, know that He is good, and that no matter what we are His forever.

One of the greatest blessings to come out of my suffering has been the privilege of being able to intercede for people who are experiencing similar situations. Someone called me one day to ask me to pray for their relative who was experiencing miscarriages, etc. I hit the floor to pray and came up with a song.

PRIVILEGE

A plea for prayer for you came across my phone line just today
Can't say I was stunned; I just didn't know what to say
Didn't know what to say

I got down on my knees and went to a place I don't often travel
To retrieve a day of a broken heart to help my thoughts unravel
Help my thoughts, help my thoughts unravel.

What a privilege, what a power has come my way
What a blessing and what an honor
It is to pray.

Though I've walked on through the years,
and I've left my loves with Jesus
Living requires we wipe the tears but the pain doesn't leave us
It doesn't leave us
Memories and feelings they lie sealed in a tear-shaped vault
Saved for special occasions to help us pray as we ought
Help us pray, as we ought.

What a privilege, what a power has come my way
What a blessing and what an honor
It is to pray.

What a purpose—What a passion
He's given me today
What a blessing, what an honor
It is to pray.

No matter what you or a loved one may be facing today, I pray that one day you will look back and be able to say, "Satan may have meant it for evil, but God meant it for good, to bring about the salvation of many people."

Hold to the Master's hand.
He's holding on to you.

CPSIA information can be obtained at www.ICGtesting.com
Printed in the USA
LVOW07s1639290715

448055LV00001B/2/P